WORLD'S CUTEST
HORSES & PONIES
in 3D

Horses and ponies have been a part of people's lives for thousands of years. Today, they are beloved pets, kept for their talents as sports horses, or for the hard work they do on farms. Show horses live a life of luxury, while working horses are prized for their strength, power, and stamina.

CONTENTS

There are many different breeds of horses and ponies. They are all related to other equines (the name for the horse family), such as zebras and donkeys. Their early ancestors lived up to 55 million years ago and had toes instead of hooves.

RED AND BLACK

Horses can be a whole range of colors, but horse breeders divide them into two main groups with special names for the different shades. Red horses include bay, chestnut, and all the brown and cream variations. Black horses are less common. A horse with black skin will often have dark and white hairs making it look gray. Horses that look white are classified as grays!

APPALOOSA

Appaloosa is a breed of horse that has a distinctive spotted pattern like a leopard. They usually have stripes on their hooves and a white ring around the edge of their eye.

DAPPLED GRAY

Certain horses start life as one color and then turn gray, often when they lose their foal coat. Some, like this one, pass through a dapple stage with dark rings which have pale centers.

PINTO

The white and colored patches on these animals make them pintos. They are sometimes known as piebald (black and white) or skewbald (any other color).

CHESTNUT
These horses are reddish brown. They can be very dark (described as liver colored) or pale, but the middle shade of sorrel is the most common for a chestnut.

PALOMINO
Palominos are a beautiful golden color, sometimes darker, with a distinctive white mane and tail.

BUCKSKIN AND BLACK
Buckskin horses are a creamy-colored variety of bay. Black horses can fade to a brown shade in the summer sun.

DID YOU KNOW?

A foal is often a much paler
color than it will become
when it gets older.

COLOR CODED
Many horse lovers think that sorrel horses are flightier than other colors of horse, and that black horses tend to be slow-natured and sleepy. Sorrel and chestnut horses make up over a third of registered American Quarter horses, while black ones are less than 5 percent.

MAKING THEIR MARK

Not all horses and ponies are a single color all over. Many of them get their character (and cute factor!) from markings that make them look different. Horse breeders have special names for the white markings on a horse's face and legs.

BAY HORSES
Reddish-brown horses, known as bay horses, always have a black mane, tail, and legs. The edges of the ears are also black.

PONY PORTRAIT
This horse has face markings that almost join together. It has a star and stripe on its forehead, a blaze, and snip on its muzzle.

GROWING UP
A horse's markings are there when it is born. They don't change as the horse grows older. This foal will have the same "bald face" marking when it grows up.

Horses can get sunburned skin, especially on the pinky skin under white markings.

LEG WEAR
Leg markings are stockings or socks. Socks stop below the knee. A small white mark around the hoof is called a coronet.

UNDERCOAT
The skin underneath white hair is usually pink.

WHO ARE YOU?
These horses are the same color but have different markings so you can tell them apart. Purebred horse markings are recorded to help identify them at horse shows.

STAND OUT FROM THE CROWD
Bay horses have black "points" as part of their natural color. They can also have individual white markings, like the one on the left, which has a star on its forehead.

DID YOU KNOW?

Sometimes, when a horse has a marking over its eye, the eye might be blue instead of brown.

HORSE TALK

Horses lovers may use words that you haven't heard before. Horses have specific names for their colors and markings, as well as their body parts. These are known as the "points" of a horse.

CONFORMATION

A horse is built to run fast or for long distances. Its body shape is called its "conformation". Horses are bred with the conformation needed to be strong, fast, or have a lot of stamina.

EYE SEE!

Horses' eyes are on the sides of the head, not the front. This helps them to see things sneaking up from around them, but they have to move their head to see things that are close. They can also see separately with each eye!

NEW WORDS
Some horse words are based on the Latin word for horse, which is "equus" (say "eck-wus"). For example, horse sports are known as equestrian sports.

JUST THE JOB
A horse's legs may look thin, but they are strong and powerful. They allow it to stop, start, turn very quickly, and to push off into a graceful jump over an obstacle.

DID YOU KNOW?
A horse's hooves are actually its toes.

BODY FACTS
A horse walks on its toes, like cats and dogs, not on its whole foot, like a human. The "withers" are where the neck and back join, below the bottom of the mane.

FACE FACTS
The hair that grows forward between a horse's ears is its forelock. Its soft nose is the muzzle, with large nostrils that let it breathe in plenty of air when it is moving quickly. Its nostrils are sometimes called "nares".

RUNAWAY!

A horse's body is designed to keep it safe in the wild. Horses are prey animals. That means they are possible food for predators hunting for meat. Horses are designed to escape rather than stand and fight. That's why they don't have sharp claws or teeth. They have to be able to run faster than the animal chasing them.

DID YOU KNOW?

Domesticated horses often wear shoes to protect their hooves. The shoes are usually made of metal and fixed in place by a blacksmith.

TALL AND SMALL

Horses and ponies are measured in hands. One hand is 4 inches (101.6mm). They are measured from the ground to the withers, where the neck meets the back. The tiniest horses are Falabellas, while breeds like the Shire Horse and Percheron are enormous!

BIG BELGIAN
One of the largest horse breeds is the Belgian draft horse. The tallest ones stand over 19 hands (76 in., 193 cm) high. They can be seen at state fairs pulling heavy loads because they are very strong.

SMALL IS BEAUTIFUL
These Shetland ponies are only foals, but even when they are fully grown they won't be more than 11 hands high (44 in., 111.7 cm).

SUPER SHIRE
Shire horses grow very tall. Males can be more than 17 hands (68 in., 172.7 cm) high. They are easy to recognize because of their height but also by the white feathering on their legs, which can cover their hooves.

CAN YOU SEE ME?

Shetland ponies may be small, but they are strong for their size. They can carry a rider on their back or be put in harness to pull a small cart or carriage.

HIDE AND SEEK

The Falabella is a rare breed of horse. They are usually no more than 8 hands (32 in., 81.28 cm) high. Foals are only 1 to 2 ft. (30.5 cm to 61 cm) tall when they are born. Cute!

RECORD BREAKERS

The record for the world's largest horse is often held by a Percheron. These magnificent creatures are usually black or gray. They are intelligent animals with a lot of strength and energy.

DID YOU KNOW?

Horses must be measured without shoes to get their correct official height.

SHORT BUT STRONG

Shetland ponies are popular riding ponies as they work well, are gentle, and they don't eat as much as larger horses! They are originally from islands off the chilly coast of Scotland, so they have long coats to keep them warm in winter. Their long forelock and mane protects their eyes, head, and neck in icy conditions.

DID YOU KNOW?

These cute creatures are so strong they can pull twice their own bodyweight. A large draft horse can pull only half its own weight!

SPOT THE DIFFERENCE

Many people start to ride on a pony, not a horse. But what is the difference? One easy thing to spot is the height: a pony is less than 14.2 hands (56.8 in., 144.2 cm) high. Ponies also have a different body shape with shorter legs, smaller ears, and a thick, broad body and neck. That's why a miniature horse is a horse not a pony—it has the right proportions for a horse but is very small.

DID YOU KNOW?

Miniature horses were once bred to be cute pets for kings and queens.

LONG LEGS

Miniature horses have the same body shape (known as "conformation") as their larger relatives. Their legs are long in proportion to their body. They have a fine, slim head, too.

EASY RIDER

Ponies are often used to teach children how to ride. Many of them are too small to take an adult rider.

FULL OF FEED
A pony only eats half the food a horse eats, even if they are the same weight.

HANDY HELPERS
Miniatures can be trained to assist people with disabilities. They are very good for people with dog allergies or phobias, and live longer than a guide dog, too.

LONG LIVED
Both horses and ponies can live 25–30 years on average, but many more ponies grow much older than that—some as old as 50 years.

PONY CLUB
Certain breeds are said to be ponies no matter what their height. These include Welsh ponies, Connemaras, and Quarter ponies, which are all good for learning to ride.

DID YOU KNOW?

Miniature foals generally measure between 15 and 22 in. (38 and 55.8 cm) at birth. And they are adorable!

MINI WORKERS

Many miniature horses can be traced back to European ancestors. Some were bred to work in coal mines, pulling carts full of coal in very small spaces. These days, a horse must be less than 38 in. (96.5 cm) tall to be registered as a miniature.

KEEP IT IN THE FAMILY

In the wild, horses live in herds. A herd will have the right mixture of males and females, and old and young horses. A foal is a baby horse, less than one year old. Grown-up males are called stallions, and adult females are mares.

MOM-TO-BE
A mare will be pregnant for around 11 months. Human mothers are pregnant for only 9 months.

BABY NAMES
A colt is a young male (under 4 years old). A female of the same age is a filly.

RELATIVELY SPEAKING
The mother of a foal is known as the dam, and the father as the sire. Horse breeders like to know about a foal's family history, such as whether its parents were racehorses or working horses.

DID YOU KNOW?
Foals are much more likely to be born at night.

BABY LONG LEGS
A foal's legs are nearly as long as an adult's. They are about nine-tenths their fully grown length.

GIDDY UP!
A foal can stand up less than an hour after it is born, and can trot and canter within hours. It will be able to gallop when it is a day old.

DID YOU KNOW?
A foal's teeth appear within a week of it being born.

DID YOU KNOW?
Horses are naturally preyed on in the wild, so they need to be born quickly and be able to run away soon after birth.

HORSEY BIRTHDAY
A horse's birthday is always listed as January 1 (August 1 in the southern hemisphere). So a horse born in July, 2022 will still have a birth date of January 1, 2022. Many breeders don't like their foals to come late in the year, as they will have their first birthday only days or weeks after they were born!

WORKING HORSES

Horses are given all sorts of jobs to do. Their strength makes them really useful for pulling things. Horses can be trained to work with their rider in dangerous situations, like police horses. Racehorses and show horses are worth a lot of money, and are taken care of very well.

TWO TIDY
The manes of these horses have been neatly braided. This keeps the mane tidy during show events such as jumping and dressage.

TRUSTY STEEDS
Cowboys in the 19th century relied totally on their horses. They would ride for many miles (kilometers) to round up and transfer cattle. Even today, cowboys still use horses to cover the rough terrain of the Great Plains.

WAR HORSE

The Lusitano breed of horse originally came from Portugal. It was bred to carry soldiers in war and for bullfighting.

HARD AT WORK

The Suffolk Punch is still used as a working draft horse. They are always chestnut in color but are becoming a rare breed.

DON'T LOOK NOW

Horses are easily spooked by things around them. Work horses wear blinders (also called winkers or blinkers) to stop them from getting so scared.

DID YOU KNOW?

It can cost more than $60,000 a year to keep a top racehorse.

HORSE POWER

Years ago horses pulled farm machinery, but now that machines have taken over they are more likely to pull carts, carriages, or heavy logs in forest work. They can still be seen in action at shows and on a few small farms.

HOW MUCH POWER

An engine's power is measured in "horse power"; for example, many Mustang cars have a 210 horsepower engine. James Watt, a Scottish engineer from the 1700s, first used the term to describe the power of an engine compared to the number of draft horses needed to do the same work.

DID YOU KNOW?

The world's biggest horse museum is in Lexington, Kentucky. The state is famous for its horse activities, especially the Kentucky Derby race which is held every May.

DID YOU KNOW?

Draft horses like these Belgians were used in wars to move heavy guns, pull carts of injured soldiers, and carry important generals high above the troops.

WILD HORSES

Horses haven't always lived a cozy life in a stable, or with humans caring for them. They were originally wild animals, well adapted to life on the move, watching out for predators. Their body is built for escape, and their coat is designed to see them through the toughest weather conditions.

NOT WILD
Most horses, even those that don't belong to anyone, are descended from domesticated breeds. This is why they are not "wild" in the same way as Przewalski's (say "shee-val-skees") horses.

KEEPING WARM
A horse's coat must keep it warm and dry in harsh weather. Some breeds, like Shetland ponies, have a coat that gets thicker in winter. This keeps out the cold but also stops rain from getting through to the horse's skin. In summer, the extra fur is lost.

FRINGE BENEFITS
Many horses with descendents from cold climates have a long, shaggy mane and forelock. It is thought that the hair helps to protect the neck and eyes from icy cold winds and low temperatures.

FREE TO ROAM
Exmoor ponies seem wild, as they wander freely across the moors of southwest England, but all the herds have owners.

MOUNTAIN PONY
Some breeds of pony are naturally tougher than others for coping with cold weather.

WILD THINGS
The only true wild horses left are called Przewalski's horses. They live in Asia and are almost extinct.

STICKING TOGETHER
Przewalski's horses live in herds in Mongolia and China. They are small—about 13 hands (52 in., 13.2 cm) high—and always have a pale body and dark tail and legs. Other countries have herds of part-domesticated horses living in the wild, such as the Brumby of Australia, the Mustang in the USA, and Sorraia horses in Spain and Portugal.

DID YOU KNOW?

There used to be another breed of wild horse, the Tarpan, but that became extinct in the 1920s.

DID YOU KNOW?

Wild horses like Przewalski's don't have a forelock of hair tumbling forward.

ON THE MOVE

The different ways a horse moves are known as "gaits." A wild horse has four natural paces or gaits: walk, trot, canter, and gallop. It is possible for a rider to train their horse to do other paces as well.

WALKING
Walking is the slowest gait. The horse moves one foot at a time, and keeps three feet on the ground.

TROTTING
Trotting is the next speed up from walking. In Western riding, a slow trot is called jogging. The horse moves two legs at a time, in diagonal pairs.

WILD AND FREE

Horses love to run! In the wild, they will gallop along together just for the fun of it.

DID YOU KNOW?

The fastest horses can reach top speeds of over 50 mph (80 kph).

QUICK DASH

Horses can gallop very fast, but not for too long. They will begin to tire and slow down after a mile (kilometer) or two. Like other wild animals, this top speed running is for escaping predators.

GALLOPING

Think of a race horse running its fastest and that's what galloping looks like. All four feet actually leave the ground at the same time. A horse can usually gallop at about 30 mph (48 kph).

CANTER

As the horse gets faster and starts running, it reaches a canter, or lope. It pushes off with one back leg so it always has one foot on the ground. Cantering is nearly as fast as galloping but with a different rhythm.

DID YOU KNOW?

Horses cool down after running by sweating. Most animals can't sweat.

RUNNING AWAY
Sometimes a herd will run because it is scared. A spooked horse will usually run at a lope or a canter. This allows it to stay running for longer without getting tired.

MY LITTLE PONY

Horses need lots of care and attention. So owning one is time-consuming. They like regular routine and need to be checked every day to make sure they are healthy. You will need to find time to feed, groom, exercise, and clean up after your horse.

SADDLE UP
You will need special equipment for your horse. A halter goes over his head so you can lead him or tie him up. Reins help you direct your horse when you're riding. A saddle and stirrups let you sit safely on his back.

POISONOUS PLANTS
If your horse spends time in a field, you must check that poisonous plants are removed. Some wild flowers and trees are dangerous for a horse to eat. They might be growing in the field, or within reach around the edge. These plants include crab apples, buttercups, poppies, rhododendron, milkweed, foxglove, yew, and ragwort.

CHANGING SEASONS
A horse that lives in a stable in winter should be gradually introduced to its summer field so that it doesn't eat too much grass all at once—this will make it sick

DID YOU KNOW?
Acorns (from oak trees) can be dangerous if your horse eats lots of them.

EATING GRASS
A horse has a small stomach so it can't eat large amounts all at once. It is best for horses to munch on grass or hay throughout the day. This is called "grazing". Some horses are fed grain but not all of them need it. For example, small ponies and horses that don't get much exercise.

WHO'S THERE?
Horses need exercise, and the company of other horses, so make sure your horse isn't left alone in a stable all day long.

DID YOU KNOW?

Skipping out (also called skepping out) is a quick clean up of a stall or paddock to get rid of droppings. Mucking out involves removing all the straw and replacing it with clean bedding.

TIDY UP

Grooming your horse is an important job. It will keep him clean and comfortable. It's also a good chance to check for cuts, swelling, or other problems, and simply to spend time together. A less pleasant job is "mucking out"—cleaning up horse droppings and dirty straw. Even a field needs to be tilled now and then so weeds and bad grasses don't grow.

ALL TOGETHER NOW

Horses are social animals that like to be with other horses. They love company so much they will make friends with other farm animals, like goats! Watch horses together and you will see how they nuzzle and groom each other, and "talk" with different noises and actions.

WET AND WILD
Some horses aren't afraid of water and will cross rivers and streams. Other horses have to be taught to enter water. If they see another horse going in, they are likely to become brave enough to follow.

GOOD NEIGHBORS
Horses often face each other and "groom" their friend with their teeth. This shows how much they trust and like each other.

DID YOU KNOW?
Horses can sleep standing up!

HOW YOU DOIN'?

A group of horses will sometimes put their noses together. Sharing each other's breath like this shows trust and friendship.

LEADER OF THE PACK

Horses in the wild live in herds. The herd has a leader that chooses where they go, when they travel, who eats and drinks first, and so on. The group protects one another from dangers such as predators and takes care of the young.

MUZZLE NUZZLE

Smell is important to a horse. Mothers recognize their babies by smell rather than sight.

DO YOU SPEAK HORSE?

Horses make a "nickering" noise to say hello. They do it to humans that they trust and to other horses they know. Mothers often do it to comfort their foals or to show they are worried (if the foal runs off).

HAVING A REST

Foals lie down to rest much more often than adults. An adult horse will lock its legs so it can snooze standing up, without falling over. They only need to lie down and sleep every few days. This helps to keep the whole herd safe in the wild.

HORSE TALK
A horse tells you as much with its "body language" as it does with noises. Its ears can show you whether it is nervous, angry, relaxed, interested, or afraid.

DID YOU KNOW?
A horse that is flicking its tail is likely to kick out. Stand back!

ROUNDUP

Horses are fascinating creatures. Whether you want to own one of your own or just like to go horseback riding now and then, you will have a great time around horses and ponies. The more you know about them, the more you will grow to understand them. Here are a few final, curious facts for you...

HEY, NOSEY!
Horses don't breathe through their mouth like we do. They only breathe through their nose. Their nostrils expand during exercise to take in more air.

TOUCHY FEELY
Horses can't see directly in front of them because of the shape of their face! They have whiskers, just like cats and dogs, which help the horse to judge when its muzzle is close to an object.

KEEP SMILING
A horse's teeth never stop growing!

NOT THE SAME
Many Arab horses have a different number of bones from other breeds.